GHOST

PARTICLES

i.m. Geoff Hardy

30-8-1950 to 30-4-2024

Fred
D'Aguiar

Introduction –

When I stood up and looked out across the faces looking at me…I felt afraid and said, "How do I do this?" but a voice said, "We're all with you." – Peter Roscoe, writing after Geoff Hardy's burial, 12th June, 2024

And then this…

'Sir, Mr. Hardy, Geoff' begins Fred's sequence, *Ghost Particles*. These names and roles – teacher, student, first-name familiars – shift and interact in lines of lament, of grief born in the immediate aftermath of Geoff's death, and in the gradual losing of him in the three preceding years of his ill-health. Formal and informal nomenclatures cross over each other, make something reminiscent of a three-stranded plait: of bread, perhaps, or a bracelet signifying friendship. *Ghost Particles* is poetry centred in affection, admiration, warmth, deep and familiar understanding, and, somehow, in the ongoing conversation between Fred D'Aguiar and Geoff Hardy, his youth-time English teacher at Charlton Boys Secondary School, London. It is in poetry alone that the poet seeks, as poets do, to understand, to come to terms with our greatest subjects, love and death, and to do so with vivid imagery and vibrant white space.

'…they found you by the weir…' How do we find the ones we've loved and lost, begin to incorporate grief into the everyday dragging solidities of sorrowing body, mind, and spirit? We can't find our beloved friend. He chose to take his own life by drowning in the River Severn: that force of water which rises and falls through Shrewsbury's seasons. And here we are, the ceremonies of death completed, left dumbstruck. Yet look again! Here are poems which begin to speak into those painful places. These poems utter what we cannot say.

'… not far from the bridge…' This bridge at Castlefields is not any bridge. It was Geoff's last standing place in those bright trainers, a representation of which, made by his partner, Peter Roscoe, has been photographed for the cover of these poems. The bridge is the view from his and Peter's home, and it runs across to Underdale physically, and now, for us, it runs metaphorically between Geoff's life and death, between our hopes for him and his excruciating despair. Mid-sequence, we are taken to the bridge to see for ourselves, and this is the most difficult part of the poet's conversation with his beloved teacher, but not its end. The bridge is the concrete place to which the poet will return to when he **'can bear it'**. Will he then be granted **'more time'**?

'your palms / twist as if / making sparks…' You never made anything else, Geoff. Your hands ignited the air and our thoughts. You sparked change, and mostly in the way we, the social we, think about sexual orientation, and what it means relationally: personally, politically. I was one of those changed, **'told…unequivocally, what to think,'** and I carry that change **'from you / back then / to me / here now'** and on into my work and living. Thanks to you, Geoff, so many of us can say with Fred, **'we found our own feet'**. It is fitting that proceeds from the sale of these poems are being donated to the Peter Tatchell Foundation.

'Must / you be / dead' Would that it were otherwise, yet **'wide-spread arms / embrace you.'** It helps us to hold on to each other, to hold onto this poetry.

***

'When Peter and you landed in Shrewsbury / in the 80s Shrewsbury did not know / what hit it. The old town listed a little / more to the left, seeing you two, / arm-in-arm.' For those of us lucky enough to live in Shropshire, we know the familiar sight of Geoff-and-Peter – on their bikes, on their way to a meeting, to market, to founding the Rainbow Film Festival. They've been for us a pioneer pairing, a double act, a double-barrelled most civilised of partnerships, full of light, air, colour, laughter, food, wine. **'Touchy, feely, kissy, Hardy.'** All that playfulness, all that affection for the world, never far away.

I know Fred because I knew Geoff. I know Peter because I know Fred. I'd seen Geoff speak before I met him. He was standing in for Peter Tatchell in a debate in Shrewsbury. Maybe it was at the time of the civil partnership vote in Westminster. I don't remember the motion at stake, but I can see Geoff, impassioned, explaining the hurts caused by homophobic hate crime before hate crime was recognised as such, and it changed me.

Next and fortuitously, I sat by Peter and Geoff at the Wenlock Poetry Festival. Fred was there, performing. It went as it always did with Geoff – I was on my own, and Geoff spoke to me, made me welcome in the public space, reached out to me (I'm sure he could see I was lonely). And we arranged for Fred to read at Shrewsbury Poetry one Sunday afternoon in 2013 at the time his collection *The Rose of Toulouse* was newly published. Geoff as listener, Geoff as poetry enthusiast, Geoff as enabler of talent, Geoff as counsellor, friend, role model, encourager. Geoff as braver than most of us can ever be. He's all here in these poems, our friend.

These poems, they're a **'tear in the space-time continuum'**. We cannot raise the dead, and yet Geoff is so close by. **'...soul / come close / closer'**, close enough to thank, as Peter did: *for the memories of holding hands over the decades, and the irony of holding hands on walking around Redwoods' neighbourhood, 50 years on from Pride 1972, eliciting nothing other than normal responses...it wasn't significant.*

Look, Geoff! You made it possible. Not to capture the times before psychosis, but for Fred to write the words we need to hear, though **'I know you won't come back'**. We can, however, return again and again to these poems which are brim-full with love, articulate with memory.

I think how you figure
in my life in myriad ways
baked in with my days

Sir, Mr. Hardy, Geoff

no longer
they found you by the weir
            current
                        settled
                                    weeds
police pulled you in their boat
from your hiding place
flesh
            bones
                        nails
                                    teeth
soaked
            freed your grip
                        massaged your feet
not far from the bridge where you jumped
in sight of Peter and your home
stomp ground
                        riverwalk
                                                wild
                                                            fruit
stretch of unapologetic turf
table and chairs for cakes and tea
Lennon blaring turntable stereo
            working
                        class
                                    hero

*

your palms
twist as if
making sparks

our Japanese
blossom tree
bark to show

how rubbed
wood shines
crimson

*

you cut
gangly rose
bushes way

back to shock
them you say
into bloom

*

Must
you be
dead
for all
there is
for me
to say
to you
to be
said?

*

we copy bees
track flowers

we play flowers
attract bees

we carry pollen
as ourselves

we are carried
by pollen

*

not far from the weir
you climb footbridge
railings at maybe 4am

      not long ago
      with Peter we
      joined people
      at the weir

      we watched current
      sweep trout
      this same stretch
      Severn spans

      not the same river
      twice or even
      once runs your Zen
      throwaway talk

you jump
widespread arms
embrace you

*

when I can bear it
I plan to stand
where you climbed

and stare down

The Severn
keeps you now
from us for life

we want you back
though you told Peter
I want to go but it's too final

*

for us
more time
than your

last time
until next
time

we meet
for we follow
you to what

no one knows
for sure
where all end

bodiless
spirits
free

*

zen
cereal
packet
insert

cookie
wisdom
paper
strip

from you
back then
to me
here now

*

When Peter and you landed in Shrewsbury
in the 80s Shrewsbury did not know
what hit it. The old town listed a little

more to the left, seeing you two,
arm-in-arm. The town suited.
Market on Saturday mornings.

Bakeries, fishmongers, haberdasheries,
Oxfam; the Natural Health Therapy Centre
you helped start. Bike rides in every direction.

*

Wales, your hills dip in sky.
'Wem will I see you again,'
we sing as we bike from Wem

to the Ashram in Wales. We sit
cross-legged on straw mats, clap,
chant, eat with bare hands

from a communal, veggie curry pot,
tear pages from volumes of flat bread
roti or nan, drink sweet well water.

'Wem will I see you again,'
we sing as we cycle back, pit
stop at the local, one for the road,

you say, who should go in first,
the queer or the black? And before
I answer you push inside

to hush that descends as if operated
by a dimmer switch. We welcome
silence as the third in our pariah trio.

We sing, 'Wem will I see you again.'
All the way home, not sure how
any of this happened, nor caring.

*

You wore your outside right heel down
more than your left.

You cleared your throat loudly
but never spat.
You hiked your pants with little twists;
rarely bothered with a belt.

You told us, unequivocally, what to think,
what's best for us, and made us wrestle
free to find our own feet.

In that you were like your forceful father,
though much kinder.

He asked me once exactly which page of Das Capital
I meant when I blurted something about surplus value
I'd picked-up from Marxism Made Simple.
I never spoke politics again in his company.

That wasn't you. You badgered to draw us out
of ourselves, showed us ways forward
for us to forge our own path.

Dear, Geoff: lover of wordplay, puns, echoes, you'd call this campaign season
in your absence, a general erection and say, whoever you vote for, the government
gets in. Pescatarian, composter, grey-water re-user, litter picker upper,
double-sided foolscap letter writer, ye of the 70s floor-length rainbow knitted wool scarf
Early mornings you blasted 21st Century Schizoid Man, followed by tea, followed by
Dylan, followed by Edith Piaf, followed by more tea, followed by Vivaldi.
Touchy, feely, kissy, Hardy, you loved Tom Robinson sing-alongs.
You make me summon Vera Lynn, we'll meet again, now you're gone.

Remember that time you cast off all your clothes and bathed
in a stream near Llangollen as perfect strangers strolled by…
You shopped deliberately at closing time in Blackheath Village Greengrocers
for the bruised rejected fruit-and-veg at rock-bottom prices; diced, sliced
and pitched them all into a red, cast-iron pot for your famous egg curry,
with short-grain parboiled brown rice washed down by a bargain Chianti.
Teacher, preacher, lamp and mirror, Alan Watts and Carlos Castaneda
pressed on me long before I knew my California from my cauliflower.

May you cycle country lanes that lead to epicurean teashops with varieties
of homemade cakes, and farms with honour baskets of produce
at the side of the road, and endless scenery every turn that you take.
May the kitchen for your concoctions store countless pots and pans
and every spice known to the gourmets on the other side.
May you rest in power and rise to sing and dance again
with advice and gifts for everyone, and all the time in the world
to shop at market and stop and chat with all the people that you meet.

*

wherever you are
we can't talk

whatever you cook
we can't share

whatever you need
whatever you do
I can't help you

we can't be in the same room at the same time
light and air may as well be partitioned

I see
I breathe

you can't see
you don't breathe

it takes the equivalent of the rapture for us to communicate
a tear in the space-time continuum
courage in lion before lion steps out with Dorothy to gain some

whatever you cook
save me a plate

wherever you are
whatever you need
whatever you do

I'm with you

*

How long souls take before they find new homes

they abandon bodies that birthed them

depends what light falls
where they happen

soul
come close
closer

break from flesh blood bones
earth rest stones mark

stranger you changed from what I knew

light air sky says yes your body died not you

*

Dear soul, hermit crab,
you outgrew home, now you search
for a shell that fits.

*

Lookout for hermit
crab that left its shell behind:
pearl necklace in bed

-room dresser, two flights
upriver from footbridge viewed
left out back window.

The Afterlife Café

We pull off the 101
for eats and drinks
at the Afterlife Café

there's the usual
coffee-teas-soda
fountain worm diet

the menu's encased
under glass-covered
tabletop placemats

bold modest prices
strip seconds off
our borrowed time

why is the café full
yet always seats
new customers?

we prefer a booth
and lo and behold
one frees up for us

you want what's not
on the menu – more
time and the waiter

reads your mind
and says they'll bend
their no-substitutes

rule just for you
they throw in a free
helping of curly fries

we could settle here
complete crosswords
knock back automatic

refills but more road
calls our destination
so we sidle from seat

and table we frog-march
for the plate glass door
oblivious of the diners

all who stop at the After
-life café exit willing
blank or in two minds

eyes on the sleepy road
foot on the yielding gas
we watch our past

slide up windscreen
over our grey heads
and out the rearview

you say we meaning
you're with company
or you intend this

for the living
who wonder what's
in store and the dead

who don't much care
to know what's what
or coming next

for all they wish for
from dying is to live long
enough to say yes

don't fuck with me
call me mad or bad but
yes to the Afterlife Café

Raising the Dead

spill red rum at front door
pinch sea salt over left
then right shoulder
garlic clove in breast pocket

        right step forward
        left join right
        left step back
        right join left

                inhale
                smile

clap right hand once against left
flick index finger against
clasped thumb and middle finger
left hand first then right

        rub palms together five times
        move left hand first
        clap hand left hand twice
        against right

                exhale
                smile

stamp left foot stamp right
shake both arms at your sides
shudder from head to foot
breathe out blubber lips

        all this by candlelight
        or full moon through window
        or a naked fire in the open
        or in REM sleep

                inhale
                exhale
                smile

Afterlife Café Redux

You sit eat drink all day
in the Afterlife Café

Lime labrish gaff swing sway
in the Afterlife Café

Meet bi trans lesbian gay
in the Afterlife Café

Dance sing meditate pray
in the Afterlife Café

Ditch the rich join poor play
in the Afterlife Café

Save the planet from prey profit
in the Afterlife Café

Stop the clock the glut the fray
in the Afterlife Café

Drop everything grab fun your way
in the Afterlife Café

Ghost Particles

make me glance sideways

caught in the corner of my eye

as no more than shadows

some feeling that tells me

look around for presences

I fully expect to be there

scenes I'm in that I recognize

as things I've been in before

though not for certain

phrases that take me back

back to longer scripts

people said within earshot

if not directly to me

as I went in my Guyanese ways

so I go in America from one thing

to another for the rest of my days

Postscript

Some point morning returns
Mid-city cockerels hark
cat-strafing magpies

dog trots before streets rise
flash yellow red green waves
crashing traffic high hire

I know you won't come back
I must settle with you gone
as I breathe think feel

laugh with my daughter
over some tv we take in over
supper and yes you cannot be

farther from me just as life
muscles elbows headbutts
back dead centre my routine

I think how you figure
in my life in myriad ways
baked in with my days

Fair Acre Press

First published in Great Britain by Fair Acre Press

www.fairacrepress.co.uk

A CIP catalogue record for this book is available
from the British Library

ISBN   978-1-911048-79-4

Fred D'Aguiar's previous pamphlet with Fair Acre, titled, *Grace Notes* was published in 2021. His most recent collection, *For the Unnamed* (Carcanet) and the pamphlet, *Arboretum for the Hunted* (Arc) were published in 2023. Born in London of Guyanese parents, he grew up in Guyana before returning to the UK. Currently, he lives in the US and teaches at UCLA.

Liz Lefroy is a British poet and organiser of the monthly event, Shrewsbury Poetry. *Pretending the Weather*, was winner of the 2011 Roy Fisher Prize and her most recent pamphlet, *GREAT MASTER / small boy* (2021) was published by Fair Acre Press.

Peter Roscoe, whose art is on the cover, has been Geoff's civil partner since 8am, December 21st, 2005.

Thanks to the editor of Poetry Review for publishing Raising the Dead in their Autumn 2024 issue.

Milton Keynes UK
Ingram Content Group UK Ltd.
UKHW050153270824
447354UK00008B/80

9 781911 048794